# PRE-SCHOOL LETTER SOUNDS BEGINNING

Fun-filled Activities

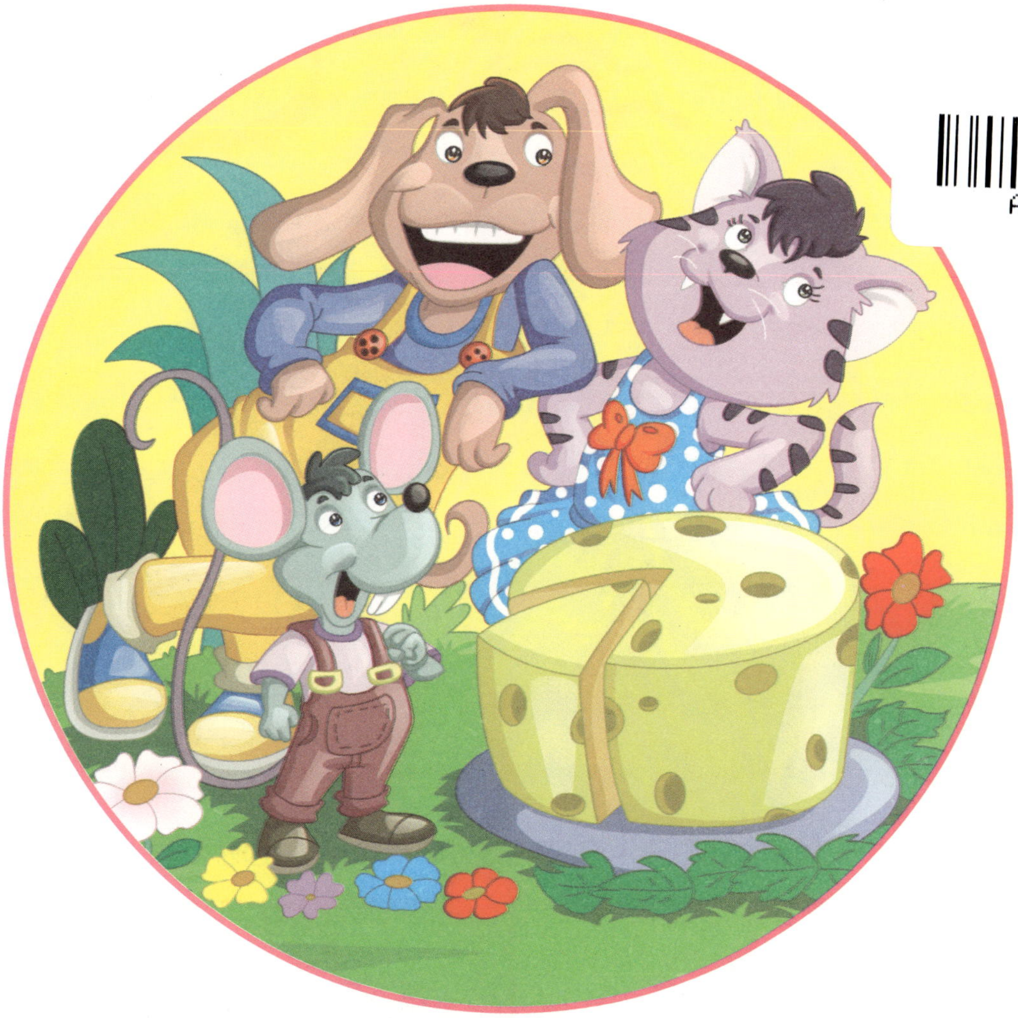



Om KIDZ
An imprint of Om Books International

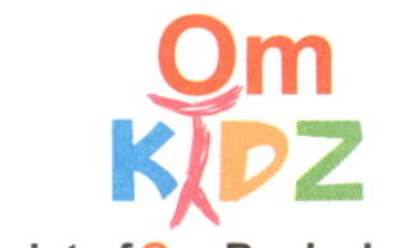

# The Letter A

A is for

Airplane

Ant

Apple

Alligator

Apron

Almonds

Circle (O) all the pictures the names of which begin with A sound.

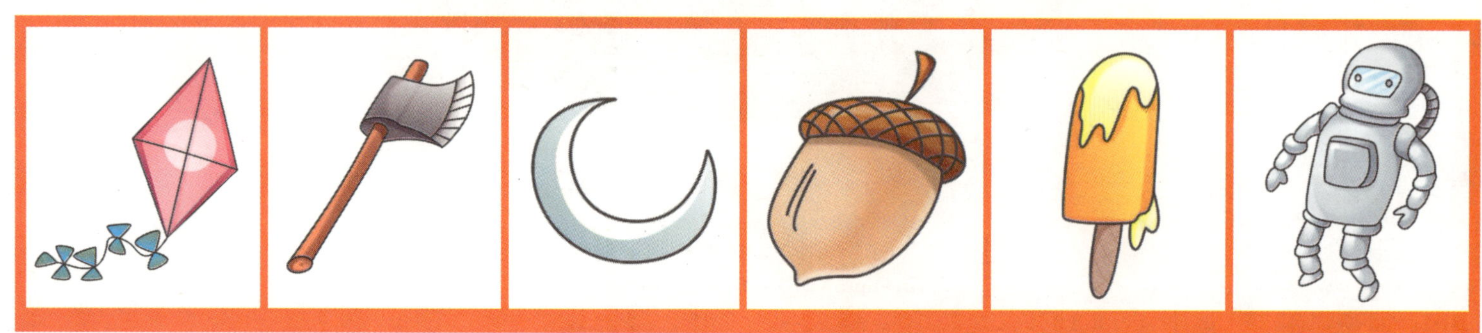

# The Letter B

B is for

Bear

Boy

Ball

Basket

Book

Boat

Tick (✓) all the pictures the names of which begin with B sound.

# The Letter C

C is for

Clock

Cactus

Curtain

Cat

Cone

Cross (×) all the pictures the names of which begin with C sound.

# The Letter D

D is for

Daisy

Dog

Drum

Dice

Doughnut

Doll

Circle (O) all the pictures the names of which begin with D sound.

# The Letter E

E is for

Eagle

Envelope

Elephant

Eggs

Tick (✓) all the pictures the names of which begin with E sound.

# The Letter F

F is for

Flag

Fishing rod

Fire

Fork

Fish

Frog

Cross (×) all the pictures the names of which begin with F sound.

# The Letter G

G is for

Giraffe

Goggles

Gift

Goose

Guitar

Grasshopper

Circle (O) all the pictures the names of which begin with G sound.

# The Letter H

H is for

Hen

Helicopter

Hat

Hanger

Hills

Hippo

Tick (✓) all the pictures the names of which begin with H sound.

# The Letter I

I is for

SWEET HOME

Igloo

Ice cream

Ink

Ice skates

Ice

Cross (×) all the pictures the names of which begin with I sound.

# The Letter J

J is for

Jet

Jaguar

Jug

Juice

Jam

Jar

Circle (O) all the pictures the names of which begin with J sound.

# The Letter K

K is for

Koala

Kite

Kettle

Kiwi

Knife

Tick (✓) all the pictures the names of which begin with K sound.

# The Letter L

L is for

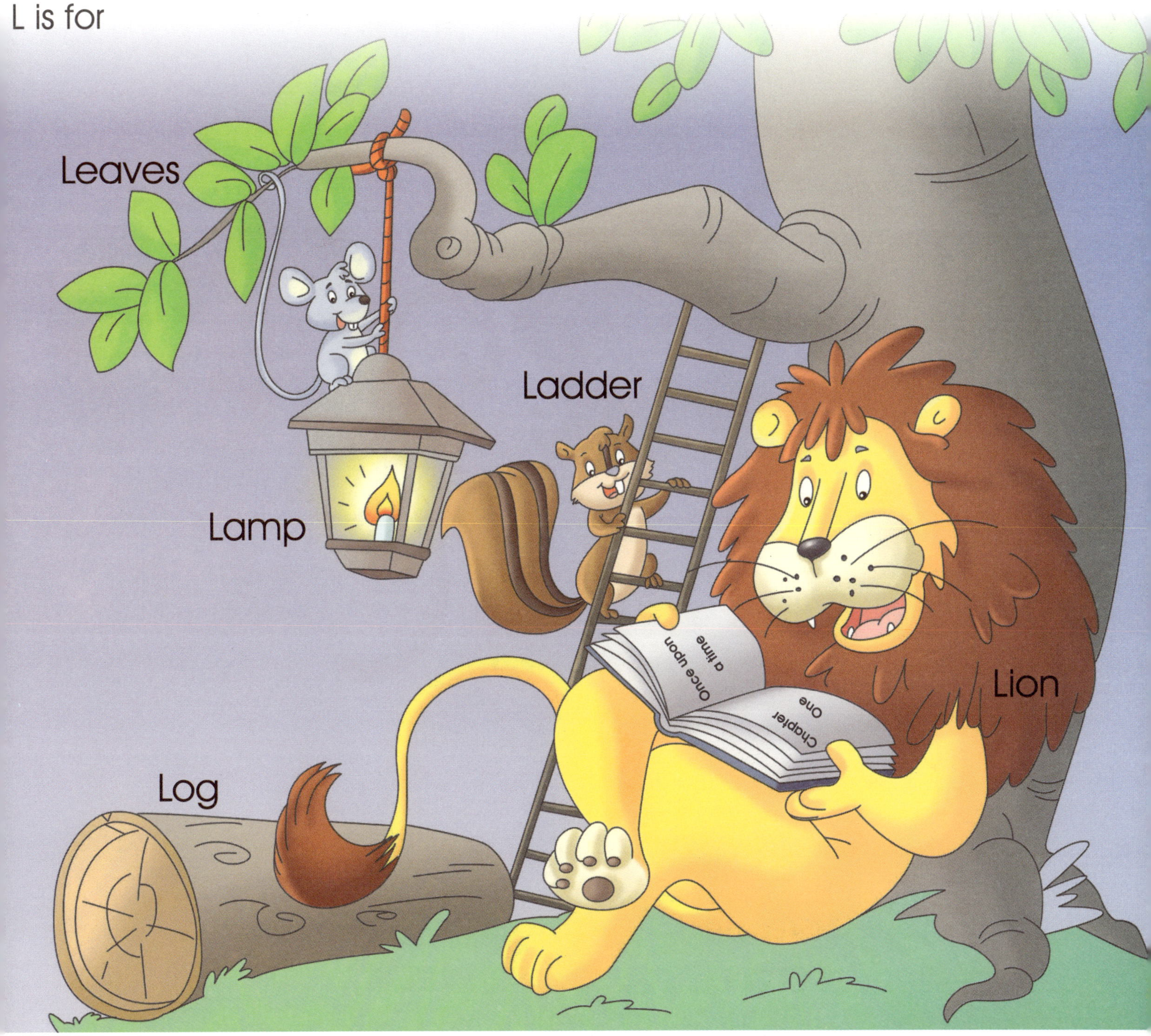

Leaves
Ladder
Lamp
Once upon a time
Chapter One
Lion
Log


Cross (×) all the pictures the names of which begin with L sound.

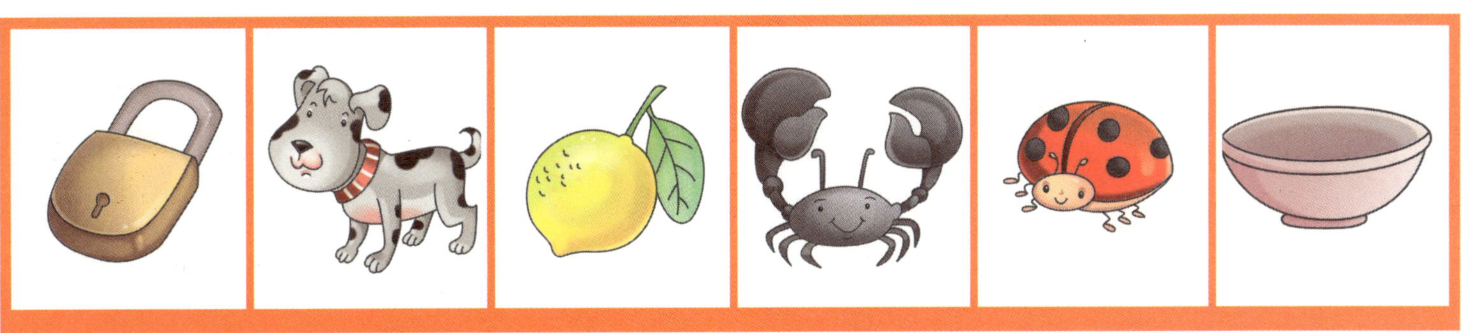

# The Letter M

M is for

Mirror

Mike

Mittens

Mat

Circle (O) all the pictures the names of which begin with M sound.

Say aloud the name of these pictures. Then write the letter with which the name of the picture begins.

# The Letter N

N is for

Necklace

Newspaper

Nest

Tick (✓) all the pictures the names of which begin with N sound.

# The Letter O

O is for

Ostrich

Orange

Octopus

Owl

Oar

Cross (×) all the pictures the names of which begin with O sound.

# The Letter P

P is for

Pencil

PEAR

Pumpkin

Pillow

Panda

Circle (O) all the pictures the names of which begin with P sound.

# The Letter Q

Q is for

Quill

Quail

Queen

Quiver

Tick (✓) all the pictures the names of which begin with Q sound.

# The Letter R

R is for

Rain

Rabbit

Rooster

Rainbow

Rose

Raincoat

Cross (×) all the pictures the names of which begin with R sound.

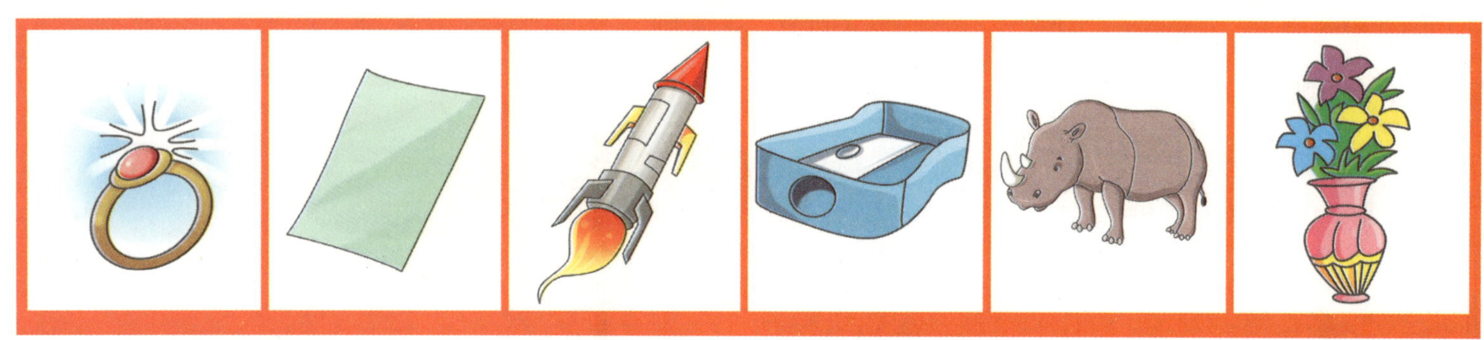

# The Letter S

S is for

Sun

Snail

Ship

Shell

Shark

Shoes

Circle (O) all the pictures the names of which begin with S sound.

# The Letter T

T is for

Toothpaste

Teeth

Tap

Tiger

Tub

Tick (✓) all the pictures the names of which begin with T sound.

# The Letter U

U is for

Umbrella

Utensils

Unicycle

Cross (×) all the pictures the names of which begin with U sound.

# The Letter V

V is for

Vulture

Volleyball

Vest

Circle (O) all the pictures the names of which begin with V sound.

# The Letter W

W is for

Wig

Whistle

Wall

Watermelon

Tick (✓) all the pictures the names of which begin with W sound.

# The Letter X

X is for

X–mas tree

Xylophone

Cross (×) all the pictures the names of which begin with X sound.

# The Letter Y

Y is for

Yardstick

Yo-Yo

Yacht

Circle (O) all the pictures the names of which begin with Y sound.

# The Letter Z

Z is for

Zebra

Zinnia

Zipper

Tick (✓) all the pictures the names of which begin with the Z sound.

Circle (O) the letter with which the name of the picture begins.

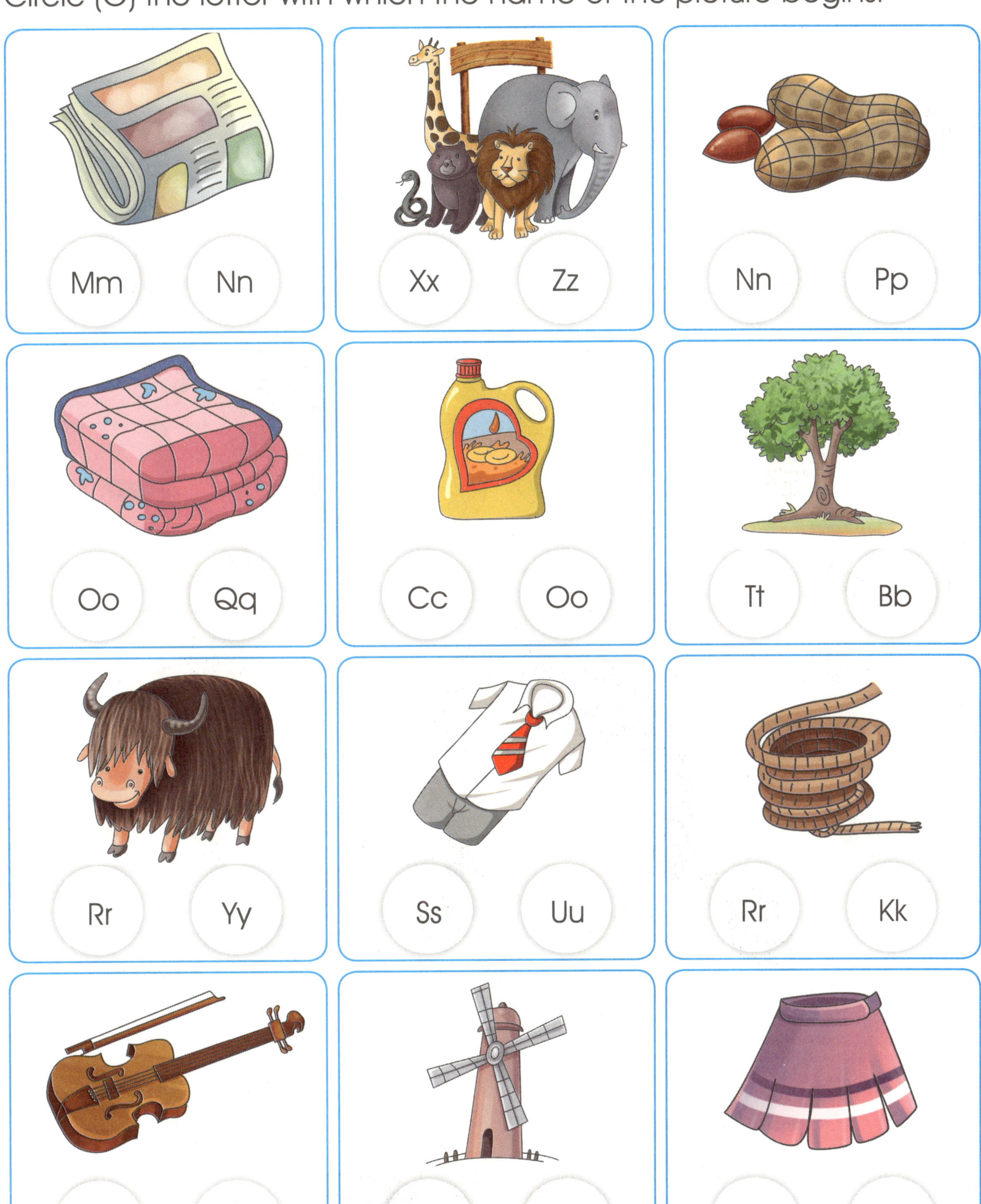

Find these hidden objects in the picture. Speak aloud their names and say the letter with which they begin.

# Answer Key

## Page 2

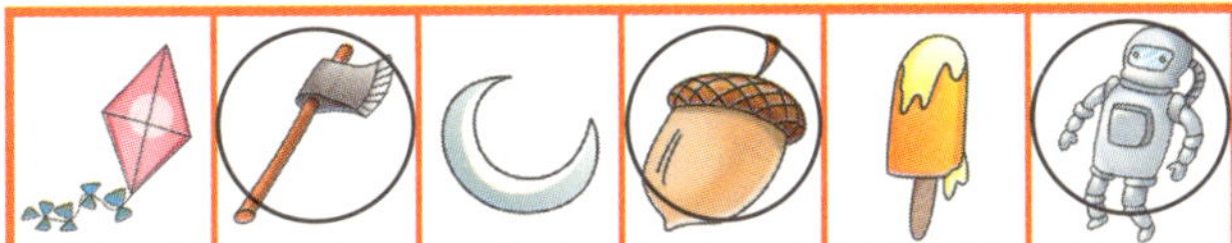

## Page 3

## Page 4

## Page 5

## Page 6

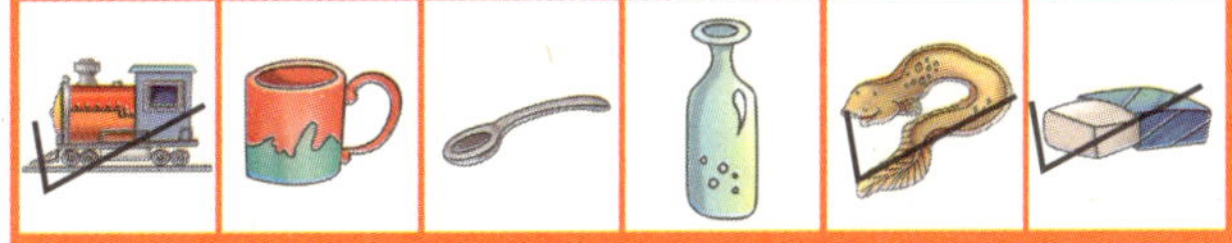

## Page 7

## Page 8

## Page 9

## Page 10

## Page 11

## Page 12

## Page 13

## Page 14

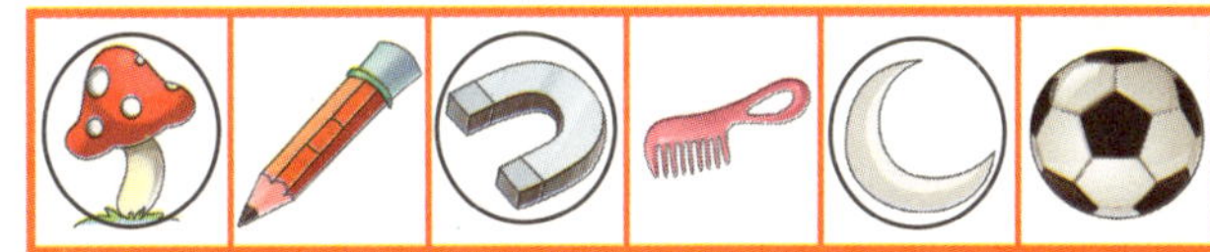

## Page 15

## Page 16

## Page 17

## Page 18

## Page 19

## Page 20

## Page 21

## Page 22

## Page 23

## Page 24

## Page 25

## Page 26

## Page 27

## Page 28

## Page 29

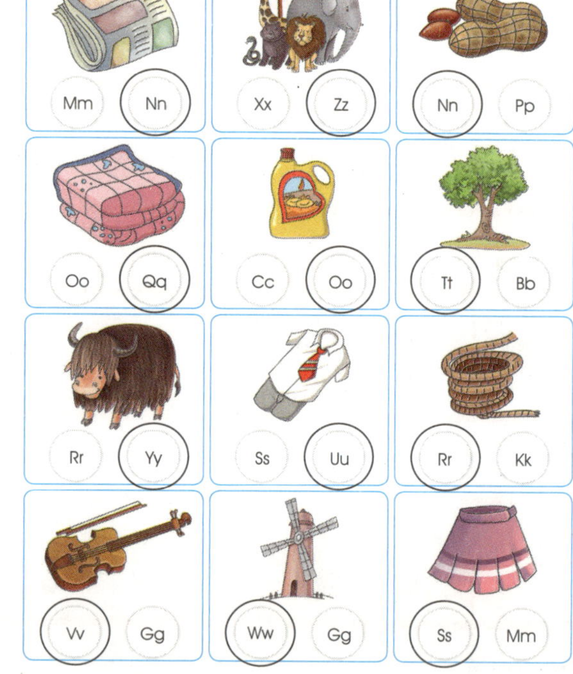


## Page 30